ICONS

SHANGHAI STYLE

SHANGHAI

Exteriors   Interiors

STYLE
Details

PHOTOS **Reto Guntli**
EDITOR **Angelika Taschen**

TASCHEN

HONG KONG KÖLN LONDON LOS ANGELES MADRID PARIS TOKYO

Also available from TASCHEN:

Inside Asia, Vol. 2
Hardcover 24 x 31.5 cm, 448 pages
ISBN 978-3-8228-4819-7

Living in China
Hardcover 26 x 30.2 cm, 200 pages
ISBN 978-3-8228-4275-1 (edition with English and German cover)
ISBN 978-3-8365-0240-5 (edition with French cover)

To stay informed about upcoming TASCHEN titles, please request our magazine
at www.taschen.com/magazine or write to TASCHEN, Hohenzollernring 53, D–50672 Cologne,
Germany, contact@taschen.com, Fax: +49-221-254919. We will be happy to send you a free
copy of our magazine which is filled with information about all of our books.

© 2008 TASCHEN GmbH
Hohenzollernring 53, D–50672 Köln
www.taschen.com

Concept, layout and editing by Angelika Taschen, Berlin
General project management by Stephanie Bischoff, Cologne
Texts by Daisann McLane, Hong Kong
Lithography by Thomas Grell, Cologne
German translation by Ingrid Hacker-Klier, Hebertsfelden
French translation by Philippe Safavi, Paris

Printed in Italy
ISBN 978-3-8365-0481-2

CONTENTS   SOMMAIRE   INHALT

The windows of Shanghai writer and diva-about-town Mian Mian's Art Apartment look out on the Huangpu River — but not for much longer. Outside, construction cranes loom over a dusty, noisy building site. "They're working so fast, it grows by one story every week. Two more months and there goes my river view."

How fast can a city grow and change? How much energy and diversity can it absorb? Since the economic liberalization of China in the 1990s, Shanghai has been setting new records in both categories. It is not the first time that Shanghai has played such a role. From 1842 to 1945, the Chinese trading city played host to an international mix of entrepreneurs and shady traders, White Russian émigrés and Jewish refugees from Nazi Germany. Entire neighborhoods bowed to the rule of a millionaire gangster, Du Yuesheng. Shanghai's architecture is as colorful, varied, and eclectic as its denizens. Along the Bund, Italianate, Art Deco and Greek Revival buildings from the early 1900s spread their

LIFE IN THE FAST LANES

Les fenêtres de l'appartement de Mian Mian, écrivain et diva mondaine, donnent sur le Huangpu, mais plus pour longtemps. À l'extérieur, des grues s'affairent au-dessus d'un chantier poussiéreux et bruyant. « Ils vont tellement vite ! Chaque semaine, l'immeuble grandit d'un étage. D'ici deux mois, je pourrais dire adieu à ma vue sur le fleuve. »

À quelle vitesse une ville peut-elle s'étendre et changer ? Combien d'énergie et de diversité peut-elle absorber ? Depuis la libéralisation économique de la Chine dans les années 90, Shanghai bat des records dans ces deux domaines. Ce n'est pas la première fois qu'elle occupe ce rôle. Dans les années 1842 et 1945, cette ville commerçante accueillait une population cosmopolite où se côtoyaient les entrepreneurs et hommes d'affaires douteux, les Russes blancs et les juifs fuyant l'Allemagne nazie. Des quartiers entiers étaient sous le joug du gangster millionnaire Du Yuesheng.

L'architecture de Shanghai est aussi pittoresque, variée et éclectique que ses habitants. Le long du Bund, des bâtiments italianisants, Art Déco et néoclassiques déploient leurs ailes. Plus loin du fleuve, des volutes d'encens s'élèvent des temples de quartiers, certains plus que millénaires. Dans les étroites allées

Die Fenster von Mian Mians Art Apartment, der Shanghaier Schriftstellerin und Szene-Königin, blicken auf den Huangpu-Fluss – aber nicht mehr lange. Draußen erheben sich drohend Baukräne über einer staubigen, lärmenden Baustelle. »Sie arbeiten so schnell, jede Woche wächst der Bau um eine weitere Etage. Noch zwei Monate, und meine Aussicht auf den Fluss ist dahin.«

Wie schnell kann eine Stadt wachsen und sich verändern? Wie viel Energie und Vielfalt vermag sie zu absorbieren? Seit der wirtschaftlichen Liberalisierung Chinas in den 1990er-Jahren hat Shanghai neue Rekordmarken in beiden Kategorien erreicht. Es ist nicht das erste Mal, dass Shanghai eine derartige Rolle spielt. Zuwanderer unterschiedlichster Nationalitäten strömten zwischen 1842 und 1945 nach Shanghai, und so lebte in der chinesischen Handelsstadt eine bunte Mischung aus Unternehmern, zwielichtigen Händlern und Spekulanten, weißrussischen Emigranten und jüdischen Flüchtlingen aus Nazi-Deutschland. Ganze Viertel beugten sich der Herrschaft eines millionenschweren Gangsters namens Du Yuesheng.

Shanghais Architektur ist ebenso bunt gemischt wie seine Einwohner. Entlang des Bundes erheben sich dem Historismus

broad shoulders. Further inland, swirling incense rises from local temples, some a thousand years old. In the narrow side lanes formed by *shikumen* – Shanghai's vernacular town houses – daily life spills outdoors, and people hang clothes, eat dumplings, tiptoe around in pajamas.

Nowadays the gangsters are gone (Du Yuesheng's mansion is now the Mansion Hotel), and the art crowd has moved in (they gather for splendid dinners under a feathered chandelier at the 52-foot-long table in collector and gallery-owner Pearl Lam's deliriously designed flat). The world's tallest building is about to debut in Shanghai's surreal Pudong area. And the party is just getting started. Join us, in these pages, for a tour through the lovingly restored Art Deco mansions, to the socialist factories-turned-luxury lofts, and the classic old lane houses, to see how this new wave of Shanghai dwellers are re-inventing the style of a great city.

formées par les shikumen, les habitations traditionnelles de Shanghai, la vie quotidienne se répand dans les ruelles : on y étend son linge, on déguste des boulettes et on vaque à ses occupations en pyjama.

Aujourd'hui, les gangsters ont disparu (l'hôtel particulier de Du Yuesheng est aujourd'hui le Mansion Hotel) et les artistes ont pris leur place. (Ils se pressent sous un lustre en plume autour d'une table de 16 m de long lors des somptueux dîners que donne la galeriste et collectionneuse Pearl Lam dans son appartement délirant). L'immeuble le plus haut du monde sera bientôt inauguré dans le quartier surréaliste de Pudong. Et la fête ne fait que commencer. Au fil des pages qui suivent, accompagnez-nous dans cette visite d'hôtels particuliers Art Déco restaurés avec passion, d'usines socialistes converties en lofts de luxe, de vieilles maisons traditionnelles cachées dans des ruelles et constatez par vous-même comment cette nouvelle vague de Shanghaïens est en train de réinventer un formidable style urbain.

verpflichtete italienisierende und klassizistische Bauwerke neben Art-déco-Häusern aus dem frühen 20. Jahrhundert. In den älteren Stadtvierteln steigen gekräuselte Weihrauchwolken aus Tempeln empor, die manchmal tausend Jahre alt sind. Im Mikrokosmos von Shanghais typischen *shikumen*-Stadthäusern spielt sich das tägliche Leben viel im Freien ab; in den engen Gassen hängt man die Wäsche zum Trocknen auf, isst seine Dumplings und spaziert im Pyjama herum.

Die Gangster sind heutzutage verschwunden (Du Yueshengs Villa ist heute das Mansion Hotel), dafür ist heute eine Kunstszene nachgerückt, die sich zu glanzvollen Banketten unter einem gefiederten Kronleuchter an der 16 Meter langen Tafel im kunstvoll-verrückten Apartment der Sammlerin und Galeristin Pearl Lam trifft.Und das Fest hat eben erst begonnen. Demnächst feiert das höchste Gebäude der Welt sein Debüt in der surrealen Umgebung von Pudong. Begleiten Sie uns auf diesen Seiten auf eine Reise durch die liebevoll restaurierten Art-déco-Villen, die in luxuriöse Lofts verwandelten, ehemaligen sozialistischen Fabrikgebäude und zu den klassischen *shikumen*-Häusern mit ihren schmalen Gassen, um zu sehen, wie diese neue Welle von Einwohnern den Stil dieser großen Stadt neu erfindet.

"…Shanghainese are traditional Chinese people tempered by the high pressure of modern life. The misshapen products of this fusion of old and new culture may not be entirely healthy, but they do embody a strange and distinctive sort of wisdom…"

Eileen Chang, author of *Lust, Caution*

«…Les Shanghaïens sont des Chinois traditionnels tempérés par la forte pression de la vie moderne. Les produits difformes de cette fusion entre culture ancienne et nouvelle ne sont peut-être pas très sains, mais ils incarnent une étrange et particulière forme de sagesse…»

Eileen Chang, scénariste de *Lust, Caution*

»… Die Menschen von Shanghai sind eigentlich sehr traditionsverbunden, aber durch den großen Druck des modernen Lebens gemäßigte Chinesen. Die missgestalteten Produkte dieser Verschmelzung von alter und neuer Kultur mögen nicht ganz gesund sein, doch sie verkörpern eine eigenartige und besondere Art von Weisheit …«

Eileen Chang, Autorin von *Lust, Caution*

EXTERIORS

Extérieurs Aussichten

10/11 Shiny new icon: the Pearl Tower, in Pudong. *Nouveau totem étincelant : la Pearl Tower, à Pudong.* Eine schimmernde neue Ikone: Der Pearl Tower in Pudong.

12/13 Along the Bund: treasure trove of early 20th century architecture. *Le long du Bund : un musée de l'architecture du début du 20e siècle.* Entlang der Uferpromenade. Der Bund: architektonische Schätze aus dem frühen 20. Jahrhundert.

14/15 The Bund: Customs House and Hong Kong & Shanghai Bank. *Le Bund : La douane et la Hong Kong & Shanghai Bank.* Der Bund: Zollhaus sowie Hong Kong & Shanghai Bank.

16/17 Wall of condos: view from Mian Mian's Art Apartment. *Des murailles de béton : une vue depuis l'appartement artistique de Mian Mian.* Eine Wand aus Appartementhäusern: Blick aus Mian Mians Künstlerwohnung.

18/19 Shanghai's changing skyline: construction site, Huangpu Riverfront. *Le profil en évolution constante de Shanghai : un chantier de construction au bord du Huangpu.* Shanghais dynamisch wachsende Skyline: Baustelle am Ufer des Huangpu-Flusses.

20/21 Ready for brunch: rooftop dining, Mansion Hotel. *L'heure du brunch : un restaurant en terrasse, Mansion Hotel.* Zum Brunch gedeckt: Man speist auf der Dachterrasse, Mansion Hotel.

22/23 Entrance to the Mansion Hotel in the French Concession. *L'entrée du Mansion Hotel dans la Concession française.* Eingang zum Mansion Hotel in der French Concession.

24/25 Courtyard of the Mansion Hotel. *Cour intérieure du Mansion Hotel.* Innenhof des Mansion Hotels.

26/27 A lane of old *shikumen*-style houses, French Concession. *Une ruelle bordée de vieilles* shikumen, *Concession française.* Eine Gasse mit alten *shikumen*-Häusern in der French Concession.

28/29 Local restaurant near Bao Yifeng's lane house. *Restaurant de quartier près de la maison de Bao Yifeng.* Einheimisches Restaurant bei Bao Yifengs Haus in einer *Long-Tang*-Gasse.

30/31 Old and new: view from Richard Hsu's house. *Le nouveau et l'ancien : une vue depuis la maison de Richard Hsu.* Alt und neu: Blick aus Richard Hsus Haus.

32/33 Backyard of Sieglinde Simbuerger's restored house near Yu Yuan. *La cour derrière la maison restaurée de Sieglinde Simbuerger près de Yu Yuan.* Hinterhof von Sieglinde Simbuergers restauriertem Haus in der Nähe des Yu-Yuan-Gartens.

34/35 Green delight: Simbuerger's courtyard garden. *Verdure luxuriante : le jardin de Simbuerger.* Grüne Pracht: Sieglinde Simbuergers Garten.

36/37 Gallery owner Elisabeth de Brabant's elegant Art Deco mansion. *L'élégante villa Art Déco de la galeriste Elisabeth de Brabant.* Die elegante Art-déco-Villa der Galeristin Elisabeth de Brabant.

38/39 Welcome to paradise: shady entryway to de Brabant's home. *Bienvenue au paradis : l'entrée de la villa d'Elisabeth de Brabant.* Willkommen im Paradies: schattiger Eingangs-bereich von Elisabeth de Brabants Haus.

40/41 Al fresco: glass French doors open on to de Brabant's garden. *Al Fresco : des portes vitrées s'ouvrent sur le jardin d'Elisabeth de Brabant.* Al fresco: Hohe Glastüren öffnen sich auf Elisabeth de Brabants Garten.

42/43 Open spaces: French doors in Pia Pierre's airy, spacious house. *Espaces ouverts : des portes vitrées dans la maison claire et spacieuse de Pia Pierre.* Offene Räume: Glas-türen in Pia Pierres luftigem, geräumigem Haus.

44/45 The wooden deck atop Richard Hsu's downtown loftspace. *La terrasse en bois sur le toit du loft de Richard Hsu au centre-ville.* Die mit Holz ausgelegte Dachterrasse von Richard Hsus Loft.

46/47 Pudong's bright lights, seen from Mian Mian's Art Apartment. *Les lumières de Pudong vues de l'appartement artistique de Mian Mian.* Die Lichter von Pudong, von Mian Mians Art Apartment aus gesehen.

48/49 Ultimate Shanghai: nighttime view, high above the Bund. *Les feux de Shanghai : le Bund vu de nuit.* Wo Shanghai am schönsten ist: nächtlicher Ausblick hoch über dem Bund.

"... in China, you can't be too radical ..."

Mian Mian, author, *Candy*

« ... En Chine, on n'est jamais trop extrême ... »

Mian Mian, écrivain, *Candy*

»... in China kann man nicht zu radikel sein ...«

Mian Mian, Autorin, aus: *Candy*

INTERIORS

Intérieurs   Einsichten

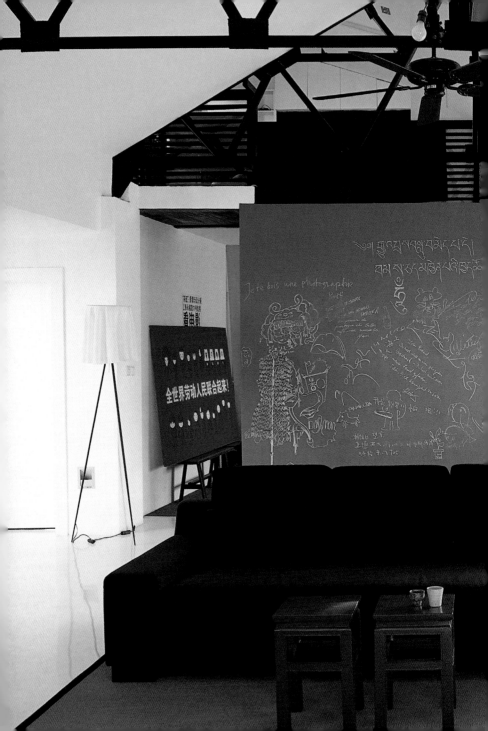

54/55 Mismatched Ming chairs at Richard Hsu's dining table. *Chaises Ming dépareillées autour de la table de salle à manger de Hsu.* Unterschiedliche Ming-Stühle zusammengestellt an Richard Hsus Esstisch.

56/57 In a glass house: another view of Hsu's dining area. *Dans une maison de verre : une autre vue de la salle à manger de Hsu.* Im Glashaus: eine andere Ansicht von Hsus Speisezimmer.

58/59 Shanghai Modern: Richard Hsu's kitchen and living space. *Le modernisme shanghaïen : l'espace séjour et la cuisine de Richard Hsu.* Shanghai modern: Richard Hsus Küche und Wohnbereich.

60/61 Hsu's room divider is also a blackboard for guests' messages. *Chez Hsu, l'espace est divisé par un tableau noir où les invités peuvent laisser des messages.* Hsus Raumteiler dient auch als Tafel für Nachrichten von Gästen.

62/63 A breathtaking bath: oval tub in Hsu's private rooftop spa. *Un bain spectaculaire : la baignoire ovale dans le spa privé de Hsu sur son toit.* Atemberaubendes Badevergnügen: ovale Wanne in Hsus privatem Wellnessbereich auf der Dachterrasse.

64/65 Architect Teng Kun Yen's stunning loft. *Le superbe loft de l'architecte Teng Kun Yen.* Das bezaubernde Loft des Architekten Teng Kun Yen.

66/67 Teng's loft is the former Japanese Embassy in Shanghai. *Le loft de Teng est l'ancienne ambassade du Japon à Shanghai.* Tengs Loft befindet sich in der ehemaligen japanischen Botschaft in Shanghai.

68/69 Traditional Chinese calligraphy desk, at Teng Kun Yen's. *Table traditionnelle à calligraphier chinoise, chez Teng Kun Yen.* Traditioneller chinesischer Arbeitstisch für Kalligrafiearbeiten im Heim von Teng Kun Yen.

70/71 Sculptural light installation in architect Teng Kun Yen's studio. *Une sculpture lumineuse dans l'atelier de Teng Kun Yen.* Skulpturale Lichtinstallation im Atelier des Architekten Teng Kun Yen.
Photo: Mok Steve/Ten Kun Yen studio

72/73 Writer Mian Mian uses aluminum foil as a door and wall covering. *L'écrivain Mian Mian a tapissé ses portes et ses murs de feuilles d'aluminium.* Die Schriftstellerin Mian Mian verwendet Alufolie als Verkleidung für Türen und Wände.

74/75 Bicycle sculpture by Shi Jin Dian, at Mian Mian's. *Une sculpture bicyclette de Shi Jin Dian, chez Mian Mian.* Fahrrad-Skulptur von Shi Jin Dian bei Mian Mian.

76/77 Natural light: the Pearl Tower illuminates Mian Mian's Art Apartment. *Lumière naturelle : la Pearl Tower éclaire l'appartement artistique de Mian Mian.* Licht von außen: Der Pearl Tower erhellt Mian Mians Art Apartment.

78/79 Purple dreams: bedroom at Bao Yifeng's. *Rêves mauves : une chambre dans l'appartement de Bao Yifeng.* Violette Träume: Schlafzimmer im Haus Bao Yifengs.

80/81 Acid green and pink cushions accentuate Bao's living room. *Des coussins vert acidulé et roses dans le salon de Bao Yifeng.* Giftgrüne Bezüge und pinkfarbene Kissen setzen Akzente in Baos Wohnzimmer.

82/83 Lobby in the Mansion Hotel, restored home of a Shanghai gangster. *Hall du Mansion Hotel, l'ancienne demeure restaurée d'un gangster mafieux de Shanghai.* Lobby im Mansion Hotel, dem ehemaligen Haus eines Shanghaier Mafia-Gangsters.

84/85 Afternoon coffee at the Mansion Hotel. *Café dans l'après-midi au Mansion Hotel.* Nachmittagskaffee im Mansion Hotel.

86/87 Velvet curtains and tufted silk head-board, Mansion Hotel. *Draperies en velours et tête de lit en soie capitonnée, Mansion Hotel.* In der Mitte geteilter Samtvorhang, abge-stepptes seiden Kopfteil, Mansion Hotel.

88/89 Tiffany light fixture and Qing dynasty lacquer table, at Sieglinde Simbuerger's house. *Plafonnier Tiffany et table en laque de la dynastie Qing, maison de Sieglinde Simbuerger.* Tiffany-Hängelampe und Lacktisch aus der Qing-Dynastie in Sieglinde Simbuergers Haus.

90/91 Indigo mood: art collector Sieglinde Simbuerger's stairwell. *Humeur indigo : l'escalier de la collectionneuse d'art Sieglinde Simbuerger.* Stimmung in Indigoblau: das Treppenhaus der Kunstsammlerin Sieglinde Simbuerger.

92/93 Sieglinde's home is also a gallery for friends' artwork. *La demeure de Sieglinde sert également de galerie pour les œuvres de ses amis.* Sieglindes Haus dient auch als Kunstgalerie für die Bilder ihrer Freunde.

94/95 Thrift shop finds in the yellow guest bed-room, at Sieglinde's house. *Dans la chambre d'amis jaune, des trouvailles chinées chez les brocanteurs, maison de Sieglinde.* Flohmarkt-schnäppchen im gelben Gästezimmer von Sieglindes Haus.

96/97 Vintage red leather club chair, at Sieglinde's house. *Un vieux fauteuil club en cuir rouge dans la maison de Sieglinde.* Roter Vintage-Lederklubsessel in Sieglindes Haus.

98/99 Chinese character for "blessing" dominates Pia Pierre's living room. *L'idéo-gramme chinois signifiant « bénédiction » domine le séjour de Pia Pierre.* Das chinesische Symbol für »Segen« beherrscht Pia Pierres Wohnzimmer.

100/101 Marble fireplace and Ming chairs in archeologist Pierre's house. *Une cheminée en marbre et des chaises Ming dans la demeure de l'archéologue Pia Pierre.* Marmorkamin und Ming-Stühle im Haus der Archäologin Pia Pierre.

102/103 A birdcage, Buddhas and opium pipes accent Pierre's sitting area. *Dans le coin salon de Pia Pierre, une cage à oiseaux, des bouddhas et des pipes à opium.* Ein Vogelkäfig, Buddha-Figuren und Opiumpfeifen bilden in Pia Pierres Sitzecke interessante Akzente.

104/105 A painting by Liu Wen Quan, at Pia Pierre's. *Un tableau de Liu Wen Quan, dans la maison de Pia Pierre.* Ein Gemälde von Liu Wen Quan bei Pia Pierre.

106/107 Shanghai deco desk, at Pia Pierre's. *Un bureau Shanghai Déco, chez Pia Pierre.* Ein Shanghaier Art-déco-Schreibtisch bei Pia Pierre.

108/109 Antique statue of a Chinese official, at Pia Pierre's. *Une statue ancienne d'un fonctionnaire chinois, chez Pia Pierre.* Antike Statue eines chinesischen Würdenträgers bei Pia Pierre.

110/111 Original brick walls add warmth, at Pierre's. *Les murs d'origine en briques créent une atmosphère chaleureuse, maison de Pia Pierre.* Originale Ziegelwände verleihen Pia Pierres Heim eine warme Atmosphäre.

112/113 Original art deco mouldings adorn high ceilings, at Elisabeth de Brabant's. *Les hauts plafonds sont ornés de leurs moulures Art Déco d'origine, chez Elisabeth de Brabant.* Die hohen Wände in Elisabeth de Brabants Haus sind mit originalen Art-déco-Stuckleisten verziert.

114/115 Embroidered Chinese *qi pao* robes decorate Elisabeth de Brabant's bedroom. *Des robes chinoises brodées,* qi pao, *décorent la chambre d'Elisabeth de Brabant.* Bestickte chinesische *qi pao*-Roben schmücken das Schlafzimmer Elisabeth de Brabants.

116/117 A soaking tub shaped like a *qi pao*, in Elisabeth de Brabant's bathroom. *Une baignoire en forme de* qi pao, *dans la salle de bains d'Elisabeth de Brabant.* Eine Badewanne in Form eines *qi pao* im Badezimmer Elisabeth de Brabants.

118/119 Ante-room in Pearl Lam's dazzling 1,000-square-meter apartment. *Antichambre de l'éblouissant appartement de 1000 m² de Pearl Lam.* Vorzimmer in Pearl Lams überwältigendem 1000-Quadratmeter-Apartment.

120/121 Zebra print fabrics and Danny Lane's hanging screens, at Lam's. *Des imprimés zèbre et des écrans suspendus de Danny Lane chez Pearl Lam.* Stoffe mit Zebramuster und Danny Lanes Hängeparavents in Pearl Lams Apartment.

122/123 Painting by artist He Jia, at Lam's. *Une toile de l'artiste He Jia, chez Pearl Lam.* Gemälde von He Jia in Pearl Lams Apartment.

124/125 Conversation pieces: rock sculptures by Zhan Wang, at Pearl Lam's. *De quoi alimenter les conversations de salon : sculptures en pierre de Zhan Wang, chez Pearl Lam.* Conversation pieces: Steinskulpturen von Zhan Wang bei Pearl Lam.

126/127 Artist Sui Jianguo's *Mao Suit* and Aarnio's Bubble Chair, at Lam's. *Le « costume Mao » revu par l'artiste Sui Jianguo et une chaise Bubble d'Aarnio, chez Pearl Lam.* »Mao Suit« des Künstlers Sui Jianguo und Aarnios Bubble Chair im Apartment von Pearl Lam.

128/129 A feathered chandelier lights Pearl Lam's 52-foot-long dining table. *Un lustre en plumes éclaire la table de salle à manger de seize mètres de long, chez Pearl Lam.* Ein gefiederter Kronleuchter erhellt Pearl Lams 16 Meter langen Esstisch.

"…The past is forever with me and I remember it all…I hear again the slow whirling of the ceiling fan overhead; I see the white carnations drooping in the qianlong vase on my desk…the silk brocade of the red cushions on the white sofa gleams vividly…"

Nien Cheng, author of *Life and Death in Shanghai*

«…Le passé ne me quitte jamais et je n'ai rien oublié…J'entends encore le lent ronronnement du ventilateur de plafond ; je revois les œillets blancs commençant à se faner dans le vase Qianlong sur mon bureau…Le brocart de soie des coussins rouges sur le canapé blanc brille toujours autant…»

Nien Cheng, écrivain, *Vie et mort à Shanghai*

»… Ich trage die Vergangenheit immer bei mir, und ich erinnere mich an alles … Ich höre wieder das langsame Surren des Ventilators an der Decke, ich sehe die weißen Nelken, die ihre Köpfe in der Qianlong-Vase auf meinem Schreibtisch hängen lassen … der Seidenbrokat der roten Kissen leuchtet auf dem weißen Sofa …«

Nien Cheng, Autor, aus: *Life and Death in Shanghai*

DETAILS

Détails   Details

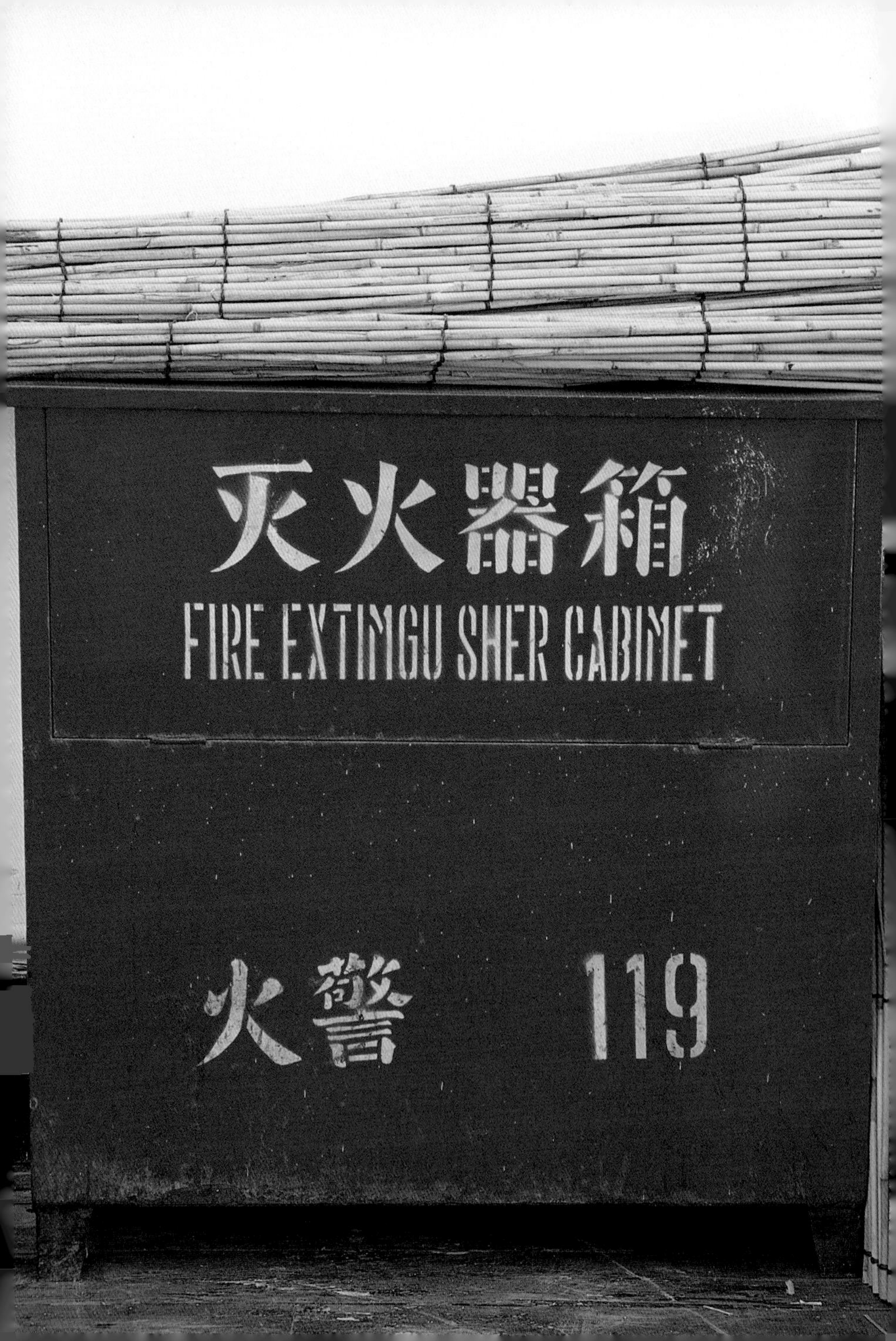
灭火器箱
FIRE EXTIMGU SHER CABIMET
火警 119

客梯　　货梯

136 Through the porthole: Huangpu River view from Teng Kun Yen's loft. *Par le hublot : le Huangpu vu de l'appartement de Teng Kun Yen.* Durch das Bullauge: Blick von Teng Kun Yens Loft auf den Huangpu-Fluss.

138 Metal lantern at Teng's house. *Lanterne en métal chez Teng.* Laterne aus Metall in Tengs Haus.

139 An old straw fedora, entryway of Pia Pierre's house. *Un vieux chapeau en paille, entrée de la maison de Pia Pierre.* Ein alter Fedora-Strohhut im Eingangsbereich von Pia Pierres Haus.

140 Ancient meets kitsch: Chinese horse and porcelain pigs. *Mariage de l'ancien et du kitsch : cheval chinois ancien et cochons kitsch en porcelaine.* Antikes trifft auf Kitsch: chinesisches Pferd und Porzellan-schweinchen.

142 Eye of the tiger: Scroll and Qing dynasty table, at Pierre's. *L'œil du tigre : rouleau et table de la dynastie Qing, chez Pia Pierre.* Das Auge des Tigers: Rollbild und Tisch aus der Qing-Dynastie bei Pia Pierre.

143 Ming dynasty calligraphy panel and Japanese sake jar, at Pierre's. *Panneau calligraphié Ming et jarre à saké japonaise, chez Pia Pierre.* Tafel mit kalligrafischen Schriftzeichen aus der Ming-Dynastie und japanischer Sake-krug bei Pia Pierre.

144 Chinese ink brushes on Teng Kun Yen's calligraphy desk. *Pinceaux chinois sur la table à calligraphier de Teng Kun Yen.* Chinesische Tusch-pinsel auf Teng Kun Yens Kalligrafie-Schreibtisch.

146 Floating stairs to second level of Hsu's apartment. *Des marches flot-tantes menant au second étage de l'appartement de Hsu.* Schwebende Stufen führen auf die zweite Ebene von Richard Hsus Apart-ment.

147 View from the sleeping loft at Richard Hsu's place. *Vue depuis la chambre à coucher en mezzanine de Richard Hsu.* Blick aus dem Schlafzimmer von Richard Hsu.

149 Washing hands over Shanghai's rooftops, at Hsu's. *Chez Hsu, on se lave les mains en contemplant les toits de Shanghai.* Händewaschen bei Richard Hsu hoch über den Dächern von Shanghai.

150 Chinese "Lion Dance" mask, at Hsu's. *Masque chinois de la « danse du lion », chez Richard Hsu.* Chinesische Löwen-Tanzmaske bei Richard Hsu.

151 Acid green glass bowl by Bořek Šípek, at Pearl Lam's. *Coupe en verre vert acidulé de Bořek Šípek, chez Pearl Lam.* Gift-grüne Glasschüssel von Bořek Šípek im Apartment von Pearl Lam.

152 Peter Ting's "Double Buddha Hand" plateholder, at Lam's. *Un porte-assiette « deux mains de Bouddha » de Peter Ting, chez Lam.* Peter Tings »Double Buddha Hand« – Tellerhalter in Pearl Lams Apartment.

154 Mao goes Grecian in Sui Jianguo's sculpture, at Lam's. *Michel-Ange version maoïste, sculpture de Sui Jianguo, chez Lam.* Mao auf Griechisch: Skulptur von Sui Jianguos in Pearl Lams Apartment.

155 Contrasts: contemporary Chinese art and Qing dynasty table, at Lam's. *Contrastes : art contemporain chinois et table de la dynastie Qing, chez Lam.* Kontraste: zeitgenössische chinesische Kunst und Tisch aus der Qing-Dynastie bei Pearl Lam.

156 Chinese goddess Kwan Yin, at Pearl Lam's. *La déesse chinoise Kwan Yin, chez Pearl Lam.* Die chinesische Göttin Kwan Yin bei Pearl Lam.

158/159 Front and back detail, hand-embroidered chair with twin bats, at Lam's. *Vue de face et de dos : une chaise tapissée d'une étoffe brodée de deux chauves-souris, chez Lam.* Vorder- und Rückseite eines handbestickten Sessels mit Zwillingsfledermäusen bei Pearl Lam.

160 Feathered chandelier, from Pearl Lam's XYZ Design line. *Lustre en plume appartenant à la ligne de design XYZ de Pearl Lam.* Gefiederter Kronleuchter aus Pearl Lams XYZ-Designlinie.

162/163 *East Venus No. 1* and *2*: sculptures by Luo Xu at Pearl Lam's. *East Venus N° 1 et N° 2 : sculptures de Luo Xu chez Pearl Lam.* »East Venus« Nr. 1 und 2: Skulpturen von Luo Xu in Pearl Lams Apartment.

164 Plush velvet chairs in the lobby, Mansion Hotel. *Confortables fauteuils en velours, hall, Mansion Hotel.* Plüschsessel in der Lobby des Mansion Hotel.

166 Grand Hyatt: Accordion windows add drama to the dining area. *Grand Hyatt : l'effet spectaculaire des hautes fenêtres en accordéon dans la salle à manger.* Grand Hyatt Hotel: Harmonika-Fenster verleihen dem Restaurant eine dramatische Note.

167 Calligraphy headboard in a guest room, Grand Hyatt hotel. *Tête de lit ornée de calligraphie dans une chambre, hôtel Grand Hyatt.* Kopfteil mit kalligrafischen Schriftzeichen in einem Gästezimmer im Grand Hyatt Hotel.

168 Vintage curved wooden railing, outside Teng Kun Yen's. *Le vieil escalier en bois de l'immeuble de Teng Kun Yen.* Geschwungenes Holzgeländer im Treppenhaus von Teng Kun Yens Wohnhaus.

170 Fire fighting equipment outside Teng's apartment. *Equipement anti-incendie devant l'appartement de Teng.* Behälter für Feuerlöschgeräte vor Tengs Apartment.

171 Vintage Mao poster in Bao Yifeng's dining room. *Ancienne affiche de Mao dans la salle à manger de Bao Yifeng.* Ein Vintage-Mao-Poster in Bao Yifengs Esszimmer.

172 Chinese warrior figure, at Bao Yifeng's apartment. *Statuette de guerrier chinois, appartement de Bao Yifeng.* Figur eines chinesischen Kriegers in Bao Yifengs Wohnung.

174/175 From Sieglinde Simburger's eclectic art collection: Chinese goddess Kwan Yin, and Mao. *Dans la collection d'art éclectique de Sieglinde Simburger : la déesse chinoise Kwan Yin et Mao.* Aus Sieglinde Simburgers eklektischer Kunstsammlung: die chinesische Göttin Kwan Yin, daneben ein Bild von Mao.

176 Whimsical clocktower-shaped penholder, at Bao Yifeng's. *Porte-plume en forme de tour d'horloge dans l'appartement de Bao Yifeng.* Verspielter Federhalter in Form einer Turmuhr in Bao Yifengs Arbeits-zimmer.

178 Side table made with 1920s Shanghai posters. *Une console réalisée avec des affiches shanghaïennes des années vingt.* Mit Shanghaier Postern der 1920er-Jahre gestalteter Beistell-tisch.

179 Descending the grand mahogany staircase at Sieglinde Simbuerger's. *Le grand escalier en acajou chez Sieglinde Simbuerger.* Die große Mahagoni-Treppe bei Sieglinde Simbuerger.

180 Detail of an enameled wedding tiara, at Elisabeth de Brabant's house. *Détail, tiare de mariage en émail, chez Elisabeth de Brabant.* Detail einer emaillierten Hochzeits-Tiara in Elisabeth de Brabants Haus.

182 Jade discs and Chinese calligra-phy brushes, at de Brabant's. *Palets en jade et pinceaux de calligraphie chinoise, chez de Brabant.* Durchbohrte Jade-scheiben und Kalligrafie-Tusch-pinsel bei de Brabant.

183 Tall bamboo birdcage in Elisabeth de Brabant's bath area. *Haute cage en bambou dans la salle de bains d'Elisabeth de Brabant.* Großer Bambus-Vogelkäfig in Elisabeth de Brabants Bad.

184 Satin Chinese scholar's cap with blue appliqué, at Pearl Lam's. *Bonnet d'étu-diant en satin orné d'applications bleues, chez Pearl Lam.* Chinesische Gelehr-tenkappe aus Seide mit blauen Applikatio-nen im Apartment von Pearl Lam.

186 Moment of repose: antique stone Buddha at Pearl Lam's. *Un moment de quiétude : ancien bouddha en pierre, chez Pearl Lam.* Ein Augenblick der Ruhe: antiker steinerner Buddha bei Pearl Lam.

187 Lobby elevator at Mian Mian's. *Ascenseur de l'immeuble de Mian Mian.* Aufzug in Mian Mians Wohnkomplex.

Living in China
Ed. Angelika Taschen / Photos:
Reto Guntli / Text: Daisann McLane
Hardcover, 200 pp. / € 19.99 /
$ 29.99 / £ 16.99 / ¥ 3,900

The Hotel Book.
Great Escapes Asia
Ed. Angelika Taschen / Text:
Christiane Reiter / Hardcover,
400 pp. / € 29.99 / $ 39.99 /
£ 24.99 / ¥ 5.900

Inside Asia Vol. II
Ed. Angelika Taschen / Photos:
Reto Guntli / Text: Sunil Sethi
Hardcover, 448 pp. / € 39.99 /
$ 59.99 / £ 29.99 / ¥ 7,900

"Inside Asia is certainly lavish: a two-volume, cloth-bound and gold-edged tour around the Far East's most sumptuous interiors." —*Wallpaper*, London on Inside Asia

"Buy them all and add some pleasure to your life."

60s Fashion
Ed. Jim Heimann

70s Fashion
Ed. Jim Heimann

African Style
Ed. Angelika Taschen

Alchemy & Mysticism
Alexander Roob

Architecture Now!
Ed. Philip Jodidio

Art Now
Eds. Burkhard Riemschneider,
Uta Grosenick

Atget's Paris
Ed. Hans Christian Adam

Bamboo Style
Ed. Angelika Taschen

Barcelona,
Restaurants & More
Ed. Angelika Taschen

Barcelona,
Shops & More
Ed. Angelika Taschen

Ingrid Bergman
Ed. Paul Duncan, Scott Eyman

Berlin Style
Ed. Angelika Taschen

Humphrey Bogart
Ed. Paul Duncan, James Ursini

Marlon Brando
Ed. Paul Duncan, F.X. Feeney

Brussels Style
Ed. Angelika Taschen

Cars of the 70s
Ed. Jim Heimann, Tony Thacker

Charlie Chaplin
Ed. Paul Duncan, David
Robinson

China Style
Ed. Angelika Taschen

Christmas
Ed. Jim Heimann, Steven Heller

James Dean
Ed. Paul Duncan, F.X. Feeney

Design Handbook
Charlotte & Peter Fiell

Design for the 21st Century
Eds. Charlotte & Peter Fiell

Design of the 20th Century
Eds. Charlotte & Peter Fiell

Devils
Gilles Néret

Marlene Dietrich
Ed. Paul Duncan, James Ursini

Robert Doisneau
Ed. Jean-Claude Gautrand

East German Design
Ralf Ulrich/Photos: Ernst Hedler

Clint Eastwood
Ed. Paul Duncan, Douglas
Keesey

Egypt Style
Ed. Angelika Taschen

Encyclopaedia Anatomica
Ed. Museo La Specola Florence

M.C. Escher

Fashion
Ed. The Kyoto Costume Institute

Fashion Now!
Eds. Terry Jones, Susie Rushton

Fruit
Ed. George Brookshaw,
Uta Pellgrü-Gagel

Greta Garbo
Ed. Paul Duncan, David
Robinson

HR Giger
HR Giger

Grand Tour
Harry Seidler

Cary Grant
Ed. Paul Duncan, F.X. Feeney

Graphic Design
Eds. Charlotte & Peter Fiell

Greece Style
Ed. Angelika Taschen

Halloween
Ed. Jim Heimann, Steven Heller

Havana Style
Ed. Angelika Taschen

Audrey Hepburn
Ed. Paul Duncan, F.X. Feeney

Katharine Hepburn
Ed. Paul Duncan, Alain Silver

Homo Art
Gilles Néret

Hot Rods
Ed. Coco Shinomiya, Tony
Thacker

Grace Kelly
Ed. Paul Duncan, Glenn Hopp

London, Restaurants & More
Ed. Angelika Taschen

London, Shops & More
Ed. Angelika Taschen

London Style
Ed. Angelika Taschen

Marx Brothers
Ed. Paul Duncan, Douglas
Keesey

Steve McQueen
Ed. Paul Duncan, Alain Silver

Mexico Style
Ed. Angelika Taschen

Miami Style
Ed. Angelika Taschen

Minimal Style
Ed. Angelika Taschen

Marilyn Monroe
Ed. Paul Duncan, F.X. Feeney

Morocco Style
Ed. Angelika Taschen

New York Style
Ed. Angelika Taschen

Paris Style
Ed. Angelika Taschen

Penguin
Frans Lanting

Pierre et Gilles
Eric Troncy

Provence Style
Ed. Angelika Taschen

Safari Style
Ed. Angelika Taschen

Seaside Style
Ed. Angelika Taschen

Signs
Ed. Julius Wiedeman

South African Style
Ed. Angelika Taschen

Starck
Philippe Starck

Surfing
Ed. Jim Heimann

Sweden Style
Ed. Angelika Taschen

Tattoos
Ed. Henk Schiffmacher

Tokyo Style
Ed. Angelika Taschen

Tuscany Style
Ed. Angelika Taschen

Valentines
Ed. Jim Heimann, Steven Heller

Web Design:
Best Studios
Ed. Julius Wiedemann

Web Design:
Best Studios 2
Ed. Julius Wiedemann

Web Design:
E-Commerce
Ed. Julius Wiedemann

Web Design: Flash Sites
Ed. Julius Wiedemann

Web Design:
Music Sites
Ed. Julius Wiedemann

Web Design: Portfolios
Ed. Julius Wiedemann

Orson Welles
Ed. Paul Duncan, F.X. Feeney

Women Artists
in the 20th and 21st Century
Ed. Uta Grosenick

ICONS